# Unconscious Mind Secrets

How to Tap Into the Hidden Power
of the Subconscious Mind
to Achieve Goals
and Get Stuff Done

by Max Trance

maxtrance.com

# DISCLAIMER

Nothing in this work is psychological advice, medical advice, financial advice or any other kind of advice. It is important to seek advice from an appropriately qualified medical professional whenever you have any kind of medical issue. And if you are undergoing psychological treatment, it may be best to discuss with your specialist before implementing any of the processes contained within this book.

The material in this work is for entertainment purposes only, and you may not be entertained.

Your use of the material in this work is entirely at your own risk. The author, publisher, and all other persons and entities associated with the creation of, sale of, distribution of and everything else to do with this work make no representations or warranties of any kind with regard to this work or its contents.

# Table of Contents

Introduction ................................................................1

Structure of the Human Mind................................................3

The Conscious Mind.........................................................9

The Unconscious Mind ....................................................14

How to Reprogram Your Unconscious Mind ...................................25

    The Foot in the Door ..............................................29

    The Easiest Way to Cause Change....................................33

    Start Building Your New Reality ...................................37

    The Power of Positive Resource States..............................41

    Deep Trance Identification ........................................45

Your Conscious Mind Is Important ........................................49

Conscious Automation of Your Unconscious Mind ...........................53

In Summary................................................................63

Conclusion................................................................66

Next Steps ...............................................................67

Also by Max Trance .......................................................69

# Introduction

Many years ago when I first started looking into things like meditation, self-hypnosis, and the mind in general, the stuff I could find was interesting, but there was a huge problem: Nothing I read seemed to adequately explain exactly how the mind worked.

People had all kinds of ideas, some good and some bad. It seemed like no-one really knew what was going on.

There was a very good reason for this. You see, when we're inside our own minds, it's easy to imagine that they work in ways that are entirely different to how they actually work.

If all we ever do is look at our minds from the inside and be confused by how other people respond, it can be impossible to make any progress at all.

It would be fair to say that the human mind is one of the largest outstanding mysteries of all time.

For thousands of years people from all walks of life have dedicated entire lifetimes to figuring it out. And even with all this effort, it's only in the 21st century that we're starting to appreciate how it all works.

We go through our lives being pushed around by circumstance and even by our own emotions.

It turns out that with a little understanding of what's going on it's possible to make a few simple tweaks that can lead to massive changes.

In this book we're going to cover the two big parts of the human mind. This is the model of the mind that many modern hypnotists use to get amazing results in record time.

We'll go over the purposes of the conscious mind and the subconscious mind, their differences, and what each can do.

And then I'll give you some simple processes that anyone can use to tame their own unconscious mind.

It is my intention that by the end of this book you will know how to take back control.

# Structure of the Human Mind

In order to gain an appreciation of how the human mind works, it's important to understand the underlying structures.

We begin with the brain.

The human brain is effectively the hardware that runs our mind. And it's also a lot more than that.

On top of providing a framework for our mind, the brain manages our entire system. This may include involvement in the automatic running of our bodies, the creation of hormones, and the regulation of our heart rate and body temperature. Alongside this, the brain may provide us with instinctual responses to keep us safe, and it does a bunch of other stuff.

While the physical aspects are interesting in themselves, from our perspective as mental explorers, we're typically much more interested in what we can do with the mind.

We don't really know where consciousness comes from, and its origin doesn't matter very much for our purposes here. What we do know is that our consciousness is associated with where we place our attention, and with our memory of the last few things we experienced.

**Experiments have shown that we can usually only place our attention on one thing at a time. Beyond that, we can hold about 7 things in our conscious memory.**

When we experience something, it first goes into our conscious working memory, and then is eventually shunted into our long term storage.

**A model of everything we ever experience is created and stored within the quadrillion or so neural connections within our brain.**

Now on the face of it, a quadrillion might seem like a huge number. To put this into context, a typical storage device on a modern computer is measured in small numbers of terabytes.

Or put another way, the human brain has at most about 1000 times the storage capacity of a typical modern computer.

You probably know someone who has had the experience of running out of space on their computer or phone. It happens to just about everyone.

And that's with us recording only a tiny portion of our lives.

Translating this back to the human brain, it's fairly easy to see that with only a quadrillion or so connections in which to store everything we ever experience, we don't have enough space for an accurate recording of the ongoing video feed from our eyes.

And our brains have to store a lot more than that.

On top of the dual video feed for around 16 hours every day, we have a constant stream of data from audio, touch, pain, and a whole host of other senses throughout our bodies, coupled with our ongoing thoughts.

Our brains deal with this by making many approximations. This has a similar effect to the data compression we see in computer files. Things take up less space, and there is an associated cost in terms of losing some of the information.

**Our memories are never more than a rough model of our experiences.**

Not only that, but our brains like to optimize. If we don't access a particular memory, over time the connections associated with that memory will be repurposed.

Eventually the memory fades.

And overall this is a good thing. As a rule, if we're no longer accessing a memory it's because we don't need it any more.

Beyond storing our memories, the brain also performs lots of processing. And once again, we run into physical limitations. There is so much incoming sensory data that our brain cannot process all of it without taking a few shortcuts.

These processing shortcuts lead to cognitive biases which can be exploited by those who know what they are and how they work.

**For the purposes of understanding the mind, I find it's easiest to think of our brains as doing just one thing: They are massive engines that associate stuff with other stuff.**

When we experience something next to something else, the associated neurons inside our brains become slightly more connected. And this association can be in either space or time.

If I look at my phone sitting on my desk, the model of my phone inside my mind becomes associated with that of my desk.

And when there's a sequence of events, a model forms inside my mind saying *this thing then that thing*.

This simple principle of stuff being associated with other stuff happens on all scales.

Nothing inside our minds exists in isolation.

Everything we model is made up of other models of smaller parts. For some of us, these models reach all the way down to subatomic particles and fundamental forces.

For example, our model of a phone might include models of the individual components, our understandings of the technologies involved, our experiences of phones in general, the larger environment in which that phone exists, the feelings we've experienced at the same time as we've experienced that phone and other phones, and more.

The system as a whole is big enough and complex enough that we end up with lots and lots of emergent phenomena.

Even the emotions that we feel become inextricably linked with our memories. And because most of us experience things with a range of emotions, we don't notice it happening except in certain edge cases.

We study for an exam, and can answer the preparation test questions perfectly. Then on the day of the exam, the knowledge mysteriously vanishes.

Even more mysterious, as soon as we're out of the exam room, the answers become obvious again.

The knowledge was there all along.

It's just that the exam is a unique situation and there are not as many linkages back to the information.

This is easy to deal with.

First, when working through practice exams, at the start of each question take a moment to close your eyes and see yourself sitting in the exam answering that type of question. Repeat this at the end after you've written your answer.

Take a few moments to practice calling up how you usually feel when you're taking an exam to recreate an approximation of the emotional state.

And then, when doing the real exam, if the answer tries to hide from you, close your eyes and mentally re-orient yourself back to wherever you were when studying. Notice everything you can around that, paying particular attention to your emotional state.

This effectively builds a bridge between the studying state and the taking-an-exam state.

When I do this, usually the answer returns right away. And if it doesn't, I just continue on with the exam. It's almost always come to me before the exam ends.

Broadly speaking, we refer to our overall mental condition at a point in time as being our state. This is typically dominated by whatever emotion is the strongest at the time, and our posture and physical location can also be powerful components.

When we always experience something within the context of only one state, it becomes possible to observe state dependent learning.

This is a bit of a double-edged sword.

On the one hand, experiencing strong emotions while we're learning something tends to result in it being encoded more strongly in our memory.

And at the same time, the presence of those strong emotions isolates the memories from our other states. To get the information out, it's generally necessary to at least partially recreate the state.

**The ease with which associations form within our brains is dependent upon how much importance we assign, and how many repetitions we experience.**

Our emotions tell us whether things are overall good or overall bad.

They're a shortcut, and the presence of a strong emotion is enough to make our brain sit up and pay attention.

Or put another way, emotions make things important to us.

The mind is sometimes described as being like software that runs inside the brain. This is sort of true, but not really. The mind is a lot more akin to an aggregation of everything we've ever experienced.

The entire purpose of the human mind is to help us to survive.

This point is of critical importance.

**Our brain and mind are not there to keep us happy, only to keep us alive.**

Emotions help keep us on track with staying alive since we generally prefer to do less of the things that make us feel bad, and more of the things that make us feel good.

# The Conscious Mind

Hypnotists tend to view the mind as being split into the conscious mind and the unconscious mind.

This model is not completely accurate.

In reality, there is much more of a continuum from conscious to unconscious. But it is close enough to be useful, and it's a very simple model that anyone can easily wrap their head around and start to use.

**The conscious mind is the part of the mind that we're aware of. It's what we usually think of when we think about our sense of self.**

In a sense, it's what we're thinking about right now.

And it comes with some significant limitations, and some unique benefits.

We can use our conscious mind to do logic and make plans. However it's limited by the facts that we can only focus on one thing at a time, and that we can only hold a very small number of things in our conscious awareness at once.

The conscious mind is also our fact checker. It helps us to inhibit broken information from getting into our brains. Whenever we experience something new, our conscious mind checks it to see whether it fits in with what we know to be true.

Usually we will accept information that fits in with our current beliefs and will reject anything else.

At least until we have a reason not to.

Or until someone like a hypnotist comes along and helps us to bypass our conscious filtering.

Since fact checking is conducted by our conscious mind, it's severely limited. All that's really required to bypass it is overloading it with so much information that we can't keep up.

Now it might seem that this bypass is impossible when we know what we're doing to ourselves. After all, wouldn't we notice since it's us doing it? It turns out that so long as we take the right approach, this is simply not the case.

We'll come to exactly how to do that a little later on in this book.

Before we can do that, we need to piece together an understanding of the conscious and unconscious (or subconscious) parts of the human mind.

Let's start with the simple process of making a decision.

To most of us, it seems like we make our decisions using logic. As a result, most people imagine that human decision making works on logic. This leads to the belief that we typically choose to do things using logic, and then experience positive (or sometimes negative) emotions as a result.

In reality, decision making works the other way around.

**First, we make an emotional decision that we want something. Then we use the logic and planning capabilities of our conscious mind to justify that decision and come up with a plan.**

Every marketer, salesperson, and storyteller knows this.

It's why we buy the top-of-the-line smartphone rather than the budget model even though most of us don't use any of the extra features.

In terms of emotions, our conscious mind is primarily concerned with things like happiness and satisfaction. We want to feel good. This has lots of consequences, including things like the fear of missing out, and the tendency of most people to choose to do whatever's easiest in the moment.

Luckily, our conscious mind comes with some nifty executive control functions that allow us to steer the unconscious. We can even use it to override our emotions and do things that we really don't want to do when we perceive some future benefit.

Our conscious mind can be used to initiate new learning, and our willpower can be used to forcibly build new unconscious habits.

Once we've built habits, we can easily steer them with our conscious minds. For most people, we don't have to think about it much at all if we want to tie our shoelaces. All we really need to do is decide to tie them, and the unconscious process takes over. Unless something goes wrong, we're mostly just watching the shoelaces become tied.

Even though it's us doing the tying.

Processes like translating letters into words, sentences, and ideas are even more automatic. As you're reading this, you don't have to consciously think about the individual letters at all. And unless I use a word with which you're unfamiliar, you probably don't have to consciously think about the words.

You consciously choose to read something. And your unconscious mind does almost all of the work for you on autopilot.

It's like someone else's thoughts magically enter your head.

The only real difference is that you read vastly more than you tie your shoelaces. Whereas we might tie our shoelaces a handful of times in a day, we typically read thousands to hundreds of thousands of words.

We also tend to imagine that we experience the world as it is.

In reality, our experience of the world plays out on a theatre inside our mind. Everything we see, hear, smell, taste, feel, and sense in any way is presented to us inside this theatre after passing through many layers of filtering in our brain.

Not only that, but because of the inherent delays created as chemicals react and move through our neural network, we perceive the world a fraction of a second after things actually happen.

Our perception of the world around us is heavily filtered, and delayed. This has some important implications that we'll come to later.

So in summary, our conscious mind is used for logic, planning, and fact-checking. We can use it to override our emotions and do things we don't enjoy for some perceived future benefit. And our conscious mind is how we push the go button on many of the countless habits that each of us has.

But the conscious mind also comes with some severe limitations. It's extremely slow. And our ability to do logic is severely limited. Most people have trouble parsing even a double-negative in real time.

This happens because we can only focus on about one thing at a time, and we can only hold about 7 things in our working memory at once.

In short, our conscious mind is what we typically think of as being us. It's our sense of self, coupled with our in-the-moment experience.

Even though we have memories, for the most part, we're not really aware of things that have happened previously unless we take a moment to think about them. Even our experience of our memories is us thinking about the past as we remember it right now.

To us, our conscious minds usually seem like all that there is. We tend to perceive a lot of things as happening to us, when in reality they are driven by our unconscious mind and can be brought under control.

# The Unconscious Mind

Our subconscious mind is a representation of everything we've ever experienced. Hypnotists usually refer to the subconscious mind as the unconscious mind. Other than the name, they are the same thing.

Compared to the conscious mind, our unconscious mind is lightning fast.

But it can't do logic.

And it can't make plans.

It doesn't even properly understand negation.

**All our unconscious mind can really do is blend states together and handle our memories for us.**

It also creates our dreams for us when we sleep, and allows us to operate within our current belief system.

This blending and association process is far more powerful than it might at first appear.

It allows us to form habits that automatically run just about everything we do.

And since just about everything is automated and habitual, almost all of the decisions that we make on a day-to-day basis are also automated.

If we consciously decide that we want a drink of water, we don't typically have to make any of the other decisions. Our unconscious mind directs us to fetch a glass, open the fridge, pull out the water jug, pour the water into the glass, put the jug back in the fridge, and close the fridge, all on autopilot.

It's so automatic that sometimes we put the jug back in the fridge even when it's empty and needs refilling.

This applies to just about every task we do in a typical day. Our conscious mind says *Hey! Do this thing!* and our unconscious mind automatically carries out every step involved.

For the most part, we don't have to worry about the mechanics of exactly how to do something since it's already been habituated and automated by our unconscious mind.

Automation on this level frees up our conscious mind for doing all those things we talked about previously.

Our unconscious minds also help to keep us safe. When there's an immediate threat, instinct takes over and we do whatever our unconscious habits deem to be the most appropriate response.

Often without conscious intervention of any kind.

We catch a bicycle barreling down on us out of the corner of our eye, and automatically jump out of the way before we become consciously aware of what's going on. Sometimes this happens before the bicycle even makes its way into our conscious visual field.

We accidentally drop a pan of boiling water and instinctively jump backwards out of harm's way.

Or any of a thousand other threats, small or large, that might occur on a daily basis.

One thing that I've really noticed is the difference between walking along a hiking track with and without wearing a wide-brimmed hat.

Without the hat, I never whack my head on anything.

Mysteriously though, when I'm wearing the hat, I tend to whack my head on overhanging branches every so often.

Where it gets weird is that my conscious visual experience is the same in both cases. I perceive things as looking exactly the same regardless of whether I am wearing a hat or not.

That's one of the benefits of the unconscious mind: it processes and responds to stuff that is within our field of vision, but outside of our conscious awareness.

**The primary purpose of our unconscious mind is our survival.**

As a part of this, it drives our motivation, telling us what's important. And it conserves energy by any means possible.

The unconscious mind also has a very strong tendency to keep on doing whatever it is currently doing. This means that unless we consciously tell it to do something else, we'll usually keep right on doing the same thing.

Many people fall into a daily rhythm where they cycle through the exact same process every single day. We get up, go to work, work, go home, have dinner, crash out somewhere, go to bed, and repeat. Every single day.

Sometimes for decades.

Our unconscious mind knows that when we do that particular sequence, we continue to survive, so it keeps on doing it on autopilot. That's the association process I mentioned earlier, only rather than associating things with other nearby things, we're associating habits with other habits. And it's not just at one level.

We run habits within habits within habits. For as many layers as are required.

We find it relatively easy to perform a small task within that structure, but larger tasks may sometimes feel like they require too much energy. To the unconscious mind, there's no real reason to invest that energy.

This is part of the reason why it can be quite difficult to start doing something, but extremely easy to continue doing that thing.

For example, suppose you want to go for a walk along the beach, or to the gym to exercise.

Once you've put on your boots or gym clothes, and stepped out the front door, the momentum has built up, and it's usually quite easy to continue on with the rest of the activity.

This also provides us with a simple unconscious hack we can use to bypass our underlying inertia and turn it to our advantage.

You see, what most people will do when faced with a task is intend to do the entire task. Suddenly there is a huge thing ahead of us, and it becomes difficult to do. We often end up overwhelmed and demotivated.

But at the same time, when we have a job, our morning routine tends to be something along the lines of get up, get ready for work, and then go to work.

While we might think about the stuff we're going to be doing at work, the process of getting there is largely automated.

And as a result, we tend to find ourselves at work and ready to start.

Just about every day.

This hack can be used for pretty much anything we'd like to achieve.

Rather than focusing on the task as a totality, focus only on the very first step.

If you want to go for a walk, put on your shoes and step out the front door. When we focus on tiny, easily achievable steps, the rest tends to follow automatically.

Especially once we've done it enough times to build up the habit.

Our unconscious mind functions primarily by associating stuff with other stuff.

This manifests in a variety of ways.

When we carry out a sequence of events or activities, our brain associates them with one another in a step-by-step fashion, and we build habits.

At its core, a habit is nothing more than a series of small steps that have been associated with one another in a specific sequence.

It's exactly the same process that allows us to take a huge number of sensory inputs distributed over space and time, and construct representations of objects and other things inside our mind.

Or put another way, the act of constructing a model of something we see or hear is exactly the same as building a habit.

We start to generalize these associations, and build beliefs around them. For example, we notice that every time we push a certain type of door, we have to operate the door handle first or the door will not open. And sometimes we have to pull instead of push.

As we notice each new thing, our belief system is constantly updated.

It becomes obvious to us that doors of a certain type will always work in that way, to the extent that when one doesn't, we will often test it for quite a bit longer than we should have, mostly convinced that it must be stuck. Or at least locked.

Eventually we reach a point known as unconscious competence, and things become so obvious to us that it doesn't even occur to us that others might not share this knowledge or belief.

And since only association processes are involved, this happens regardless of whether our belief is consistent with reality.

**In the unconscious mind there is no logical assessment, only association.**

This is part of the reason why our conscious mind is so important: It helps us to provide a consistency check against our current beliefs, and also against logic and our observations of reality.

Since we believe that we are filtering things adequately, most of us never take the time to question things that are already a part of our belief system.

Which means that once something makes its way through our conscious filters and into our unconscious mind, we tend to believe it to be an absolute truth.

Our unconscious mind also drives our memory.

From the inside, it can appear that we are sometimes reminded of things, but mostly have random thoughts.

While there may be some randomness at play, what's actually going on is far simpler than most might dare to imagine.

When we experience anything, whether it's our own thoughts, bodily sensations, or things out in the world, the pattern matching in our brains fires up every associated pattern to some extent.

And since we are typically experiencing millions of discrete things at any point in time, whichever of those gets the most attention tends to steer our thoughts and memory recall.

We catch a whiff of salt on the air and hear some waves rolling in, and suddenly we find ourselves thinking about a holiday at the beach we had as a kid.

We hear a few notes of a song, and suddenly the rest of the song starts playing in our head. If the song is associated with an event, we might even find ourselves thinking about that event.

This is presumably why shows have theme songs. They create continuity and familiarity, and remind the viewer of all their emotions and previous experiences around that show.

In hypnosis terms, these are known as anchors, and I cover them in a lot more detail in **Artful Hypnotic Anchoring**.

For our purposes here, the important thing is that memory recall is driven by the same unconscious association process that creates the memories in the first place.

This also means that the process of learning itself is nothing more than association on a grand scale at every level conceivable. At the fundamental level, every single thing we ever learn is nothing more than something being associated with something else inside our mind.

Unfortunately for us, our conscious minds are very limited, so it's possible for things to make their way into our unconscious mind that we'd probably prefer weren't there.

As I mentioned, we can only filter a tiny handful of things at once using our logic and reason.

Sometimes these things are obvious.

Someone tells us that the Earth is flat, and we look out over the ocean and notice that not only can we see the curve with our own eyes, but we can combine this knowledge with a couple of other points of reference to calculate the radius of the Earth using nothing more than high school mathematics.

Sometimes the things we are filtering are more complex.

We're told that atoms are these blobs with a core and orbiting electrons, and we're given a visual like a planet with some moons. It sounds plausible. And unless we dig deeper, we'll probably believe it.

Especially since not believing it requires understanding the mathematics of wavefunctions. Or at the very least, running an experiment to observe the interference patterns ourselves.

Ultimately though, these are both simple observations. If we take the time to make the observations and do a little math, it's easy to do.

There are other things we probably should be filtering that are far more insidious.

Entire classes of things exist that most of us don't even think about filtering, let alone keeping them out of our unconscious minds.

We grow up around negative people, and find ourselves with a negative outlook on life. It's abstract, so it's much harder for us to notice what's going on.

If those people are in a position of authority, the effects are magnified.

Or worse, we think lowly of ourselves.

We decide that we can't possibly succeed.

We start using words like they and them to describe what we'd like to have happen.

*They should build a cinema here.*

*They need to clear this pathway.*

*Someone else should do something about that.*

We find ourselves moving agency for things we'd like to have happen onto other, non-specific people.

And because of this, we find ourselves constantly missing opportunities.

These unconsciously-installed beliefs about our own failings tend to be known as limiting beliefs.

And the very first step in overcoming them is noticing that they exist.

Because the truth is, our brains create associations between everything we experience. And when doing so they don't distinguish very much between real physical things we observe out in the world, and emotions we absorb from others.

If we don't consciously filter stuff, it all goes into our unconscious mind.

Now there's one more thing it's important to be aware of about the way our mind works.

We perceive ourselves as experiencing the world around us.

The truth is a little more abstract. Even though it seems to us like we're experiencing the world, what we really experience is a heavily filtered representation of the world, playing out inside our mind.

This representation is shaped by our unconscious perceptual filtering, and it's also shaped by our current beliefs.

As we covered earlier, we can only hold about 7 things in our conscious awareness at once. Any more than this, and even real physical objects can be deleted from our perception.

We literally don't see something that's right in front of us.

This might sound bad on the face of it, but in reality it's mathematically required. Even with a quadrillion connections in our brain, we still have nothing like the resources necessary to process even our immediate environment, let alone all our memories from a lifetime.

So our brain makes shortcuts, and these shortcuts are what lead to us being able to be consciously aware of only a tiny handful of things at once.

Now our brain likes to optimize stuff a lot. If something seems unnecessary, the brain may try to leave it out or ignore it.

This has the interesting consequence that when something is inconsistent with our current beliefs, and we believe it's impossible, we can sometimes fail to even notice the thing happening.

Needless to say, when we don't notice something, our lack of attention does not in any way impact on the extent to which that thing happens.

Beyond that, everything we experience leaks through into our unconscious mind to some extent.

This has an important consequence: If we don't pay attention to what's going on around us, and we choose not to question anything that seems inconsistent, we can end up with internal conflicts that we don't even know exist.

All of us have at least some beliefs that are inconsistent with reality. It's impossible for us to not have them, since doing so would require far more resources than we have available.

What we can do though is use our conscious attention to shape the things that are important to us.

The truth is that our perception of reality is shaped not only by reality itself, but also by our own thoughts, beliefs, and memories.

And once we know how, those are things over which we can assert some degree of control.

# How to Reprogram Your Unconscious Mind

There's a seemingly obvious solution when we want to reprogram our unconscious mind. It's easy. All we have to do is change all the relevant associations, and we'll change the resultant beliefs and behaviors.

It's possible you can see the tiny flaw with this.

How exactly do we change associations formed over an entire lifetime?

On the face of it, this probably sounds impossible.

Like trying to drain an ocean with a teaspoon.

I mean, sure, it could technically be done.

But it would take forever.

It's possible that the ocean might refill from rivers and streams more quickly than we can drain it.

If you've ever tried to untangle a tangled thread or rope, you'll appreciate that untangling can sometimes take a lot longer than tangling.

And in a sense, our minds have a quadrillion threads.

Beyond that, we already know that when we consciously model the new stuff we want, and then act it out, it can often lead to resistance.

Luckily things are not quite as dire as they might first appear.

Sometimes using willpower is the quickest and easiest way to build a new habit. So long as we apply our focus mostly to completing just the first step, it can be quite effective.

And sometimes it seems like no matter what we do, we find ourselves not doing stuff and not making changes. Even though we've already decided that we want to do that stuff or to make those changes.

When this happens, rather than taking it as a sign that we should give up, it usually means that another approach might be needed.

It's time to tweak the unconscious mind.

Remember, all our unconscious mind can really do is look after our memories, and blend states together. This means that if we want to change the things in our lives, the process for doing so unconsciously is a lot more akin to blending hot and cold water than it is to logic.

Our unconscious mind works largely by association, so this blending applies not only to changing our habits and working towards goals, but to everything we do.

Consciously we tend to try to solve problems with logic. The issue is that this doesn't work directly with emotions. We may run through negative things in our heads over and over again. And as might be expected, quite often this only makes things worse.

Once we've learnt the underlying lesson, what we really need to do is find a way to let go.

We need a way to get the foot in the door, so to speak.

Now there is a caveat here: For any problem we face, learning how to solve it requires effort. And some problems require more effort than others. If our problem is that we'd like a glass of water, for most of us the solution is to grab a glass, go to the sink, and fill the glass with water. On the other hand, if our problem is that we need to design and build a system to safely transport drinking water to our home on demand, a lot more effort is required.

The same is true with our unconscious minds. Some things are extremely easy to fix, while others might require years of study to learn how to approach the problem.

And it's even worse. With problems in the unconscious mind, things that might seem insurmountable are sometimes easy to fix, while things that seem like they should be simple can turn out to be anything but.

Luckily there is a rule that may be applied: When you're starting out with anything new, only work on problems where you don't care about the outcome. Then slowly scale up as you build the required skill.

For every problem that you face, you get to choose whether you want to invest the time to figure out the solution, or just find someone who already knows to help you.

For most people who want on-demand drinking water in their house, the solution is to have a plumber hook them up to the local water supply. For some people, the answer is to have a contractor install water tanks, rainwater collection, purification, and all the rest. And for a small number of people, the best approach is to build it themselves.

It is exactly the same with anything we'd like to change in the unconscious mind. If you want to overcome bad habits and work towards your goals more, those are skills that everyone probably should acquire.

The reality is that we can only think a limited number of thoughts at once, so when we intentionally spend our time thinking the thoughts we'd like, those thoughts occupy more of our mind.

This is where a lot of the law of attraction stuff comes from. Rather than being some mystical process, it's just simple math applied to the behavior of the neural network inside our brain.

Through building new unconscious thinking habits, we can make it much easier for us to consciously direct our life towards the life we'd like to have.

As luck would have it, there are lots and lots of ways to modify our unconscious thinking habits. Literally everything we can do causes these changes to some extent.

The trick lies in making the changes that we want.

And the easiest way I know to make the changes we want is to build a positive resource state, and then use that to drive the change.

# The Foot in the Door

Not all change has to seem like change. In fact, for most people, we can make a start on reprogramming our unconscious mind by doing nothing more than shifting our focus more towards the positive.

One of the easiest ways to start to shift the unconscious mind towards the positive is through practicing gratitude. When we invest a few moments each day in bringing the things that are already good into our conscious focus, we tend to start to take on a more positive outlook.

And when we have a positive outlook, it's much easier to get ourselves to do things. In a way, the positivity leaks into other parts of our lives.

In short, when we practice gratitude, we not only notice or remind ourselves of the things we already appreciate, we also put out positivity into the world.

If you've not done this before, it might feel clunky and awkward at first. But that goes away quickly.

It's usually easiest to begin using gratitude by keeping a gratitude journal. This is nothing more than a notebook that you write in every day.

So find yourself a notebook, or in a pinch, open a new file on your device. Then, set aside a few minutes each day to write in it. Set an alarm to remind you to do it.

Take the time to write 3 things that you're grateful for every day. These can be anything at all, big or small. It doesn't matter if you find yourself repeating from time to time.

If you feel so inclined, add a reason.

*I love that my keyboard has Bluetooth because it means I can write on my phone almost as easily as on my computer.*

*I'm grateful that the heaters work because it's cold outside and I like to be warm.*

*I am glad that someone invented sunglasses because I love going for walks outside in the sun and I like being able to see when I do.*

It doesn't matter what you are grateful for. Just express it in a positive way.

Our goal here is automatically having positive unconscious thoughts more often. We want to make having this type of thought into an unconscious habit.

Now you might be thinking it's enough to just think these things, and that's sort of true, and sort of not true.

You see, our brains assign importance to everything we experience.

We have thousands and thousands of thoughts every day. As a result, we'd have to think something a lot for it to not be lost in the general hubbub.

We tend to spend far less time speaking out loud than we do thinking. For some of us, the only reason for this is that we just can't speak as quickly as we can think. And for most of us, we only speak out loud when we want to convey something to someone else. Or to ourselves.

Speaking out loud tends to have more of an impact on us than mere thinking, because there's less of it, so it's less likely to be lost in the background noise. Not only that, but when we speak something out loud, much more of our brain has to light up in order to do it. And we hear the outcome.

In short, it's more work for us to speak than it is for us to think.

As a result, our brains tend to assign more importance to a statement we make out loud than they do to something we only think.

And they assign even more importance to statements we make to other people.

These days, most of us type a fair amount of stuff on a day-to-day basis. But a lot of it is short-term stuff, and quickly forgotten. Regardless of how important it may seem to us at the time, overall this tells our brains that stuff we type isn't very important.

In fact, it's even worse. When we go off on a rant on some online post, it tells our brain that the post is important, even though we might not know the person in question, and even though there is no possibility for them to ever have any other impact on our life.

The end result is that for most of us, usually when we type stuff out, our brains can place importance on things that aren't at the expense of things that are.

Typing something once is probably a little more effective than saying it out loud once, because we can come back to it later.

Luckily there's another way.

These days, most of us rarely write things out by hand. Writing stuff out by hand takes a lot longer than typing or talking, so we only tend to do it when something is important. This creates an association between writing by hand, and importance.

Not only that, the act of picking up a pen and paper, and physically manipulating both of them in such a way as to produce coherent writing engages a lot of our brain. Since more of our brain is being used, it's automatically more important to us.

Put together, this means that we can artificially make things more important to our brain by doing nothing more than writing them out by hand.

I'm sure you can see where this is going.

If you want to get the best results from keeping a gratitude journal, make sure that it's a physical one. And make your best effort to write 3 things you are grateful for every day.

When we do this, we start to build a habit. Eventually it comes to feel natural enough to us that we start to automatically express gratitude to others.

And once we do that, our entire experience can begin to shift.

Building gratitude into our life like this leads to the creation of habits that ultimately lead to us taking a more positive outlook.

# The Easiest Way to Cause Change

To the uninitiated, intentionally causing change to the unconscious mind might seem like a Herculean task.

As luck would have it, there are many, many ways to go about actual implementation.

Our unconscious minds can't really do logic, so when we want to change them, the primary way we can do this is through making the new ideas important enough. And the two ways we can do that are through repeating something a lot, and attaching an emotion to it.

One way to get started is through the use of affirmations. An affirmation is nothing more than a simple, positive, present-tense statement about something we'd like, as if it were already true.

*I love going to the gym and exercising.*

*Every day I learn at least one new thing.*

*I find it easy to deliver compliments to others.*

Hopefully that's enough for you to get the general idea. It's basically the same thing as gratitude, only for stuff that's not necessarily true for us yet.

To create your own affirmation, simply choose something you'd like to be different, and then write out a statement in the present tense, just like the three examples above.

In the beginning you don't even have to believe that the subject of your affirmation is possible for you. It does have to be something you believe is possible for someone though.

So for example, the affirmation *I enjoy eating fresh fruit and vegetables* is about something that is definitely possible. A lot of people love fresh fruit and vegetables. And even people who are disgusted by them know that.

On the other hand, if your affirmation is something like *I can teleport myself instantly to the other side of the world*, no-one at all knows how to do that yet. This means that such an affirmation is unlikely to be effective, unless you happen to be a scientist conducting such research.

So choose something that people can do, and that you'd like to be true for you, and write your affirmation about that.

Next, just writing the affirmation down doesn't do very much. Unlike with gratitude where we are reminding ourselves of something that's already true, with an affirmation we are convincing our unconscious mind of something that might not be true yet.

This means that it's important to practice our affirmation in order to embed it into our unconscious mind. If we can make ourselves feel a strong positive emotion when we do it, this will help to tell our brain that it's important and we'll tend to pick it up more quickly.

Ultimately though, if we want our affirmations to become our reality, we have to say them out loud a lot. Each time we do this, the affirmation becomes a little more deeply embedded into our unconscious mind.

As it becomes more deeply embedded, we start to imagine.

And eventually, we start to believe. As a part of that, we tend to start doing things that lead towards it becoming true.

If we tell ourselves that we love going to the gym 50 times every day, sooner or later we're going to try it out if for no other reason than to see what happens. And because we've been telling ourselves that we love it, we've primed our mind be more inclined to notice the positives rather than the negatives.

Now 50 times may seem like a lot, but in reality this can be achieved with an investment of no more than a few minutes every day.

The trick lies in remembering to actually do it. In the beginning you might find it easiest to simply set an alarm. I've always found alarms to be disruptive, so what I prefer to do is create a simple hypnotic anchor.

Choose something that you do on a daily basis, such as opening a door, sitting down in a specific chair, turning on a faucet, or any of the countless other things we all do every day.

Once you've selected a specific event, consciously say your affirmation out loud as you do that thing. Go to the chair in question, sit down, and as you finish sitting down, say your affirmation out loud. Go to the faucet in question, turn it on, and say your affirmation out loud.

Each time you do this, it builds the associations inside your brain. After a little while, the affirmation will become attached to that activity, and it will start to become a habit.

And once something becomes a habit, we don't even have to think about it much. It just happens until we decide to replace it with something else.

As an aside, if others are around you can work your affirmations into conversation with them. In the worst case, even thinking your affirmations is better than forgetting about them.

# Start Building Your New Reality

It's one thing to think, write down, and say out loud the things we'd like to be true. It's quite another to make them actually happen out in the world.

For all but the simplest changes, if we want to make those thoughts into reality, we need to do more.

What we really need is a plan, and a way to make that plan happen.

One of the easiest ways to make and implement plans is to build and use the skill of visualization. We need to have a visceral experience of what it will be like when we have what we want, and we need a way to get there.

A lot of people imagine that visualization is something that's just too hard for them to do. In reality, it's easy, once you know the trick.

Some people imagine that if they can't see a full-color 3D image in their mind, they are somehow not visualizing.

With visualization, there are those who have experiences that are indistinguishable from real life. And it certainly seems to be possible to train most people to have those experiences.

The thing is, they're not necessary in order for visualization to be effective.

And the reason is very straightforward: The important thing is your own internal representation.

Visualization works because our brain gets to have an experience of something before we do it out in the world, which trains it to more easily have that experience. It doesn't matter in the slightest what experiences other people might have. All that matters is your own experience.

Since it's your own experience that matters when it comes to visualization, the best way to do it is whatever way your brain already does it.

At least in the beginning.

To discover what this might be, think about a place you are familiar with. It can be anywhere at all, so long as you've spent enough time there that you know where everything is.

Then close your eyes and imagine yourself in that location. For example, if it's your living room, allow yourself to have a sense of your sofa, your chair, your coffee table, your TV, or whatever you have in your living room.

I'm sure you get the idea.

Critically, you don't have to see anything. In your mind's eye, imagine yourself sitting in your favorite spot, picking up the remote, and working the TV.

Or doing whatever it is that you do there.

It's easy to do, right?

You can do it even if you don't see any pictures inside your mind yet.

All you need is that idea of what the place is like.

That's all that visualization is.

Sure, you can learn to do things that give you that full-color 3D representation. But it's not needed in order to make changes to your unconscious mind.

To use visualization to reprogram your unconscious mind, choose something that you'd like to be different. And then imagine what things will be like when it is different.

In your mind's eye, imagine yourself being and doing as that new version of you.

When we do this, we're starting to pattern in a new way for us to be, and it helps us to build our motivation to get us there.

Beyond that, it helps us to plan since we can more clearly see what's needed.

If you visualize yourself relaxing on the deck of a boat in the tropics, you can start to explore and notice what else might be required.

Start by asking yourself a simple question: What do I want?

And then visualize it.

Notice all the details. Pay special attention to what emotions you feel when you have that.

Look back at what was required to get there.

And build a plan.

Step by step.

This applies to everything, not just physical things like boats.

If you want to be happier, visualize what that's like to give yourself the experience.

Notice what's different. Especially the feelings.

And go from there.

# The Power of Positive Resource States

If there's one thing that helps more than just about anything else when we want to influence our unconscious mind, it's the ability to build positive resources.

The human mind exists in a series of states that are constantly flowing into one another.

In this context, a state is nothing more than our full mind-body experience at a point in time.

For convenience, we tend to give states nifty labels which help to make them easy to identify.

These labels include things like happy, confident, cheerful, sad, miserable, excited, enthusiastic, and energetic, along with many more.

And because these are mind-body states, every mental state we experience tends to have a corresponding way that we hold our body.

Now, if you go up to a random person in the street and ask them to feel a specific way, most people can't really do it. Especially if they are in a state that's very different from the one you've asked for.

When someone's feeling down or upset, and we tell them to cheer up or be happy, most of the time the outcome is that they become more annoyed.

But if we acknowledge their current state, ask for permission, distract them a little, and then ask them to do something that we know will move them towards that state, most people can do that.

So long as happiness is currently appropriate for them, the problem isn't that they don't want to be happy. It's that they don't really know how to do it without a little guidance. And, of course, most people don't like being told what to do.

The same is true with your own unconscious mind. Once you know a few simple tricks, it can become almost effortless to shift your state at will.

Of course, you still have to remember to do it.

There are three simple tricks that we can use to quickly and easily build resource states.

Before you begin, take a few moments to allow your mind to clear. There are lots of ways to do this. In a pinch, just grab anything in your immediate physical environment, and spend a few moments noticing the details.

For example, I have a glass on my desk right now. I can reset my state to a neutral one by picking it up and spending a few moments doing nothing more than noticing its details. It has a series of ridges around the base, so it clunks a bit as I rotate it on the desk. Moving in discrete steps. The surface of the glass is almost smooth, but with a tiny amount of bumpiness.

There are other details.

I'm sure you get the idea.

Do not rush this part. Depending on what state you're in to begin with, it might take a couple of minutes to return to neutral.

Once your mind is clear, you're ready to begin.

First, since body posture is tied directly into state, physically move into a posture that goes with the state you'd like to build.

Just this simple act will tend to move us towards experiencing the new state we'd like.

Next, think back to a time when you felt the feelings you'd like to be a part of your resource state. Inside your mind, go deep into the experience of remembering what that was like.

As human beings, we cannot hold a state for more than about 2 minutes without doing something to keep it going. And since we need to get rid of our old state in order to create the new one, initially you may have to hold the pose and think about those memories for a full 2 minutes before your state starts to properly shift.

Finally, as your resource state is approaching peak intensity, do something to remind you of it. This can be as simple as seeing a symbol in your mind, tapping the back of your hand, or anything else at all you can make happen and can observe.

The key is to choose something that is unlikely to come up in your day to day life unless you intentionally will it to do so.

In hypnosis, this reminder is known as an anchor.

And as with everything else we learn, quite often we have to repeat the process a few times to make it stick. Start off with 3 repetitions, and then scale up or down from there as needed.

Once it seems like it's working, return yourself to your neutral state, and then do the thing that reminds you of your resource state. This is known as firing the anchor.

When you've built it enough, the anchor will be linked to the state, and the act of firing the anchor will cause you to return to the resource state. Usually.

As with everything, practice is required.

For best results, write out a few positive states that you'd like to be able to use as resource states. These can be anything at all. To give you some ideas, most people find things like determination, confidence, and so on, to be helpful.

Once you've selected a handful of states, choose an anchor for each and write it down so that you don't forget.

Then work through the process for each to recreate the state and attach it to your chosen anchor.

# Deep Trance Identification

Ericksonian Hypnosis is full of very cool ideas. One of the nicest of them is the idea of Deep Trance Identification.

With Deep Trance Identification, we take on some of the properties of another person, creature, or anything else at all, for a time. This gives us a fresh perspective, and it can allow us to automatically take on traits without having any conscious idea of how we're doing it.

Traditionally this is done by going into a state hypnotists tend to refer to as deep trance, imagining what it's like to be whatever or whoever we are identifying with, and then acting like and experiencing the world as if we were that person or thing for a time.

In short, we're imagining and pretending to be someone or something else. Only from a place of hypnosis.

It's even possible to take on some of the skills of people we admire, without having to go through the usual process of learning and practicing.

Naturally this doesn't apply to all skills. If you don't know anything about physics, no amount of imagining that you can think like Einstein or Heisenberg is going to magically turn you into a physicist.

And if you're already a physicist, deep trance identification with any physicist you admire is likely to give you fresh insights.

Your baseline knowledge is an important part of what kinds of things might be easy for you to pick up through deep trance identification.

For most of us, this means that it can apply to a lot of skills.

These skills include all of those that can be learnt by unconscious observation. And a huge number of skills can be learnt in this way.

Let me give you an example.

Anyone who can communicate and structure information could theoretically give a presentation on stage about a topic where they have knowledge. Since you've made it this far through this book, that definitely includes you.

Even if it's just being on the stage and conveying something like *The human mind can be considered to be comprised of a conscious part and an unconscious part.*

Or what you had for breakfast.

Depending on your skill as a presenter, your presentation could be world class, or it could be dull and incomprehensible. Or anywhere in between.

Since presentation is something that we can easily observe and it's a skill that all of us already have to some degree, it tends to be fairly amenable to being improved with deep trance identification.

In your mind's eye, see a presenter you admire. If you can't think of any, you can easily find recordings of most online and watch those to get an idea.

So see the presenter you admire in your mind's eye. If you know how to hypnotize yourself, go into self-hypnosis and step into a hypnotic reality based on their stage.

And if you don't know self-hypnosis, it's fine to just imagine for now.

Close your eyes, and imagine that you are that person you admire. Using the visualization we discussed earlier, see yourself on their stage.

Think about that person and notice details about them. Notice what's important about the particular skill and how they do it.

In the case of presentation, it's going to be oriented quite a bit around their body language, posture, and manner of speaking.

How do they stand?

How do they move?

Do they pause often when they speak?

Do they speak quickly? Or slowly?

Go deep inside what it's like to be that person.

See yourself being on their stage and giving your presentation as they might do it.

And then orient yourself into your own body, and still acting as if you were that person, deliver your presentation as them.

When we do this, we start to build unconscious habits that cause us to take on the parts of their skills and behaviors that we most admire.

The best part is that you can do this for just about any skill. As I mentioned earlier, it's important that you have the necessary baseline knowledge. But once you do, the sky is the limit!

Beyond that, deep trance identification can be used to bring in parts from your future self.

If there is some way you'd like to change, take a few moments to imagine what you will be like when you're that new version of you.

How do you act?

What kinds of things do you think about?

How do you hold yourself?

Ask yourself questions about what's important towards becoming that new you. It doesn't matter if you don't get it right, or if you move in the wrong direction. For now, just assume you will notice and change course as needed.

It's a bit like going to the supermarket. It doesn't matter if you walk in the wrong direction initially, so long as you have some way of noticing and changing course.

The key is to get moving first, and then make course corrections as you go.

So step deeply inside your imagination of that new you.

The you you'd like to be.

Each time you do this, a little more of that new you will come back with you to the present.

# Your Conscious Mind Is Important

There's an interesting thing about the unconscious mind. It drives just about everything we do. But if we want to make changes to it of our own choosing, we have to exert conscious effort to do so.

And that means that if we want to get anywhere, we need to ensure that we design plans for our conscious mind as well.

That process begins with asking ourselves a simple question: What do I want?

Naturally each of us will have many answers to this question.

What we want is not a fixed thing, but something that evolves over time.

If we're thirsty, what we want right now is probably something to quench our thirst. And when all of our basic needs are met, our wants tend to expand beyond those needs into other ways we can improve our lives.

Sometimes these improvements are trivial and immediate. We just want to be entertained for a bit, so we read a book or binge the latest show on our streaming provider.

Other times they are deeper and longer term. We decide that we want to acquire a new skill, go on an extended trip, get that promotion at work, or buy our dream home.

Or anything else we choose.

Whatever it is that you want, the very first step is noticing that you want it.

And once you've noticed that you want something, you need a way to get it.

Ultimately, in order to achieve any kind of long term goal, we need some kind of plan.

Not just any plan though. To be effective, plans have to make logical sense in the world. If you want to go on that extended trip, at the very least you really need to figure out some way to fund it.

Beyond making sense in the world and actually being designed to lead towards your goal, plans have to also be something that your conscious mind can get onboard with and carry out.

What's needed is a way to make most of the actual work in carrying out the plan happen automatically, while our conscious mind gives the occasional nudge to keep us on track.

Before we get to how to make plans happen automatically, there are three things we need to cover.

First, it's of vital importance to appreciate that the best plans should change over time. The reason for this is very straightforward: When we are in the planning phase, we don't usually know everything that could possibly go wrong.

When something goes wrong in our plan, that entire step might need to be rewritten from scratch. It's even possible that all subsequent steps have to change along with the one that broke.

So when creating plans to get you to your goals, start out with only the big steps.

For example, my plan to go cruising has steps like learning how to repair boats, deciding what kind of boat I want, acquiring the necessary certifications, and a few others.

Every one of these steps has many sub-plans.

I find that it's best to view every plan in the same way as I view science experiments. There's an outcome I want, but I can't really fail. All that can ever happen is I move closer to my goal, or I learn something new, which also moves me closer to my goal even if not in the way I had expected.

The key is to make your plans to achieve your goals as minimal as possible, while leaving in all the important steps.

Coming back to my boat example, it wouldn't really make sense to include learning outboard motor maintenance in my plan until I have reached the conclusion that I will need an outboard motor and will need to be able to service it.

Next, it is essential to keep yourself on track. In short, we need a way to bring ourselves back onto task when we become distracted.

And a big part of this is making sure that we actually enjoy the process. One easy way to do that is to have a celebration every time we achieve something.

Now you might be imagining that I mean throwing a party.

Nothing could be further from the truth.

The important thing is creating a positive association with the actual work of carrying out the plan.

This is extremely easy to do. Remember when we were talking about creating positive states and anchoring them earlier? All you have to do is create a state you enjoy and associate it with something you can do.

Even things like that feeling of satisfaction at a job well done are enough.

The key lies in taking a moment to appreciate what you've just accomplished every time you achieve something that moves you towards your goal.

Anchor that feeling of satisfaction to something you can easily do, such as smiling and nodding, and then take a moment to fire that anchor and appreciate your progress. Every single time.

When the celebration is tiny like this, it's possible to have many of them every day.

And naturally, you can add in actual big celebrations for the bigger steps if you like that kind of thing.

Finally, if you want to achieve your goal, it is essential to set aside time to work towards it. How you do this depends on you and your schedule.

Here's the reality: If your plan is likely to require 1000 hours to complete, and you do not set aside a specific time each day to work on it, it's probably not going to get done.

Which brings us nicely back to habits.

# Conscious Automation of Your Unconscious Mind

It's all very well to know that we want something badly and to be highly motivated towards getting it. But the thing about motivation is that it requires willpower to get us to do things.

And using willpower is draining. You see, we only ever have to use willpower to do things that we don't want to do in the moment.

When we rely on willpower to achieve our goals, what tends to happen for most of us is that we run out of energy and motivation, and even start to resent the thing that we previously enjoyed and were looking forward to.

Luckily there's a much easier way.

All we have to do is build some habits.

That's part of the reason why it's important to set aside some time every day. Now when I say every day, it doesn't have to actually be every day. There are other life constraints. But it does have to be regular and consistent.

It might be that we can only spare the time on Sunday to work towards our goals.

Whatever your personal schedule might be, set aside some time at the same point in every cycle.

Work out exactly what happens immediately before each time you will work towards your goal.

As an example, if you work a regular office job and find yourself crashing on the sofa after dinner every night, you might choose that as a suitable time to slot in working towards your goal.

Earlier I mentioned how we have a certain amount of mental inertia. It's generally easiest for us to keep on doing whatever we're doing, and it's harder to do something different.

The way to overcome this is to repurpose the start of the thing you want to stop doing, as a trigger that fires your habit of working towards your goal.

So in our example above, we would want the act of sitting in the sofa to automatically trigger us to continue working towards our goal.

And conveniently, because of how our minds work, this is very easy to set up. All we have to do is practice a few times.

Imagine yourself getting home from work and doing the getting-home-from-work things, whatever those might be. Then physically sit in the sofa, take a moment to briefly feel a sense of accomplishment about what you've already achieved, consciously notice yourself doing it for a moment, stand up, and take the first few steps towards working on your goal.

Once this process has been repeated enough times, the act of sitting in the sofa in that context will become just one more step in the habit of coming home from work and starting on your goals.

Naturally, you'll want to substitute your own specific circumstances rather than just blindly sitting on my imaginary sofa.

So far as I can tell, the vast majority of things that we do in our lives are driven in this manner. All we're doing here is noticing and then turning the system to our advantage.

But what if there were a way to enhance that natural process beyond what we've already discussed?

As it turns out, anchors tend to set more solidly when we create them from a place of hypnosis.

Let me tell you a story.

A few weeks ago, I noticed that I was consuming what might be considered to be slightly too much chocolate.

Now, I love chocolate, but I deemed that it had to be done.

So first I mapped out what I was doing. Pretty simple, right?

I was getting up regularly, wandering to the chocolate stash in the kitchen, taking one or four, going back to my desk, and then consuming them.

Naturally my desk is not going to be a helpful anchor here since I sit down at it and get up from it many times every day.

My first attempt was to redirect the anchor on the bowl containing the chocolates.

I walked to the bowl, smiled and nodded, grabbed some chocolates, and went back to my desk.

Not quite the desired outcome.

So I tried again. This time around, I went into self-hypnosis first, walked to the bowl, smiled and nodded, intentionally reached for the chocolate, and willfully stopped my arm mid-flight. I paused for a few seconds reflecting on that. Then I retracted my arm and went back to my desk.

Success!

Well... not quite.

I'd managed to do the thing, but I hadn't yet habituated it.

And there was no failsafe.

Reflecting on what had happened, and all the other habits I've successfully changed in the past, I decided that I probably needed 3 levels of failsafe.

If I grab the chocolate, I should release it automatically.

If I reach for the chocolate, my arm should stop mid-flight.

And ideally, if I am going for chocolate, something should stop me before I even start to reach for it.

That sounds like a plan. So naturally, I had a chocolate to celebrate.

Gosh darn it!

Clearly it was time to implement the plan.

So I went into hypnosis, visualized myself reaching for the chocolate, picking it up, pausing to really notice the experience of holding the chocolate, and dropping it back in the bowl. Three times.

Then I walked to the chocolates, picked one up, noticed all the sensations around that for a few moments, dropped the chocolate, allowed myself to feel satisfied for a moment, and walked back to my desk.

I repeated that physical process a couple of times to be sure.

After a few rounds I could feel the act of dropping the chocolate becoming automatic, so I moved on to the next one.

Still in hypnosis, I returned to my desk, and visualized myself walking to the chocolates, reaching for a chocolate, pausing mid-flight, allowing myself to go deep inside the sensations in my arm as it was stuck like that, then retracting my arm and returning to my desk chocolate-free.

Again, I repeated a few times, and then physically acted it out until I could feel the process starting to become automatic.

Almost there now!

Back to my desk, once again I visualized myself intending to get a chocolate, walking to the kitchen, seeing the chocolate bowl, pausing, noticing the internal tension for a few moments, and then returning to my desk.

Rinse and repeat.

I acted out the physical process until it felt automatic.

And just like that, it was done.

It was a few weeks ago that I did this, and since then I have had zero chocolates.

As I had anticipated, in the beginning, I would get all the way to the chocolates and would actually grab one before dropping it.

After a few days, I was at the point where I would stop and turn around on seeing the bowl.

And now, after just a handful of weeks, I don't even bother to get up and go looking for chocolates any more.

And the best part about all of it is that I can still eat and enjoy a chocolate if I so choose. It's just that now it is a matter of conscious choice rather than an unconscious habit.

Since I know how habits work, as of the time of writing I have not yet chosen to have one.

It is exactly the same with every goal you want to achieve. The easiest way I know to ensure that you actually do the required things is to choose a trigger point in the things you already do and intentionally link that trigger point to working towards your goal.

You sit down on your sofa, notice the sensations, get up, and start working towards your goal. Except that you use your own trigger point that fits into your life in place of my imaginary sofa.

Now you might have noticed that I've mentioned self-hypnosis a few times here. That's because the truth is that when we focus intently on anything we're doing, we can learn much more quickly.

There are lots of places you can learn self-hypnosis, including my book **The Self-Hypnosis Formula**. How much of it you need depends to some extent on what you are doing with it.

In this case, we want to use self-hypnosis to help us build a habit as quickly as possible. The same process works without self-hypnosis. It just takes longer.

So to get you started, here is a very simple process you can follow to induce self-hypnosis.

1. Close your eyes.

2. Focus all of your attention on one part of your current experience. I find that focusing on all the sensations within a hand or foot can work well here.

3. As you're focusing, pay attention to all the details you can. If you're focusing on your hand, notice all the temperatures, pressures, positions, and other sensations. When we place enough attention on our hands, we can literally feel the air flowing past as we move them even very slowly. Move your hand quickly enough to notice the air, then slow it right down until it is barely moving and you can still notice that sensation.

4. Continue for 2 to 3 minutes.

5. Open your eyes while still noticing those sensations.

As you repeat this process in the right way, you should find that it becomes easier and quicker. And after a short while, most people reach the point where they can shift their attention to their hand, immediately notice the air and other sensations as they are barely moving it, and find themselves in hypnosis.

You might be wondering how to get yourself out of hypnosis again. I find that it's best to not worry about that. Most people fall out of hypnosis within 2 minutes of when they stop actively trying to maintain the state. And the worst case is that you fall asleep and wake up back in your regular state.

We all go in and out of self-hypnosis many times every day without even thinking about it. All we're doing here is teaching ourselves to make that happen on demand.

So far we've covered the practical steps to getting your conscious mind onboard with achieving your goals. In summary, decide what you want, make a realistic, high-level plan for getting it, choose a time when you will regularly work on your plan, and then consciously turn something you already do at that time into a trigger for your habit of working on your plan.

If we want something to stick inside our mind, we have to tell our brain that it's important. And the easy way to do that is through the use of repetition and allowing ourselves to feel positive emotions.

Now there's one final point that it's critical to touch on. How do we know when to quit?

Because the truth is that not all plans can work. Sometimes this will become obvious as soon as we try to implement them. Other times we need to carry out some of the steps first.

What we definitely do not want to do is continue working on a plan once we know with certainty that it cannot succeed.

At this point you need to rely on your judgment. How big is the goal you are going for?

I'm quite literally making this up, but a not-unreasonable expectation is that for most goals, if you've worked through 10% of your plan, you should be starting to see some results.

For example, with my plan to go sailing, I can see clear results in that I now know how to sail and I know how to repair just about everything that could fail on a boat.

There was a time when I did not have those skills.

And here's the thing: As soon as I tried to steer my boat into its berth and missed, and then figured out how to fix that on the very next sail, I knew that I was making progress.

The key is to work out what's a reasonable amount of time, and then scale accordingly.

If your plan is going to take several lifetimes to complete, there's a good chance that you might need to make some changes to the plan.

And if you thought your plan was going to take a year, but after a month you can see it will actually require 2 years, you get to decide whether to invest that time and effort or move on to something else.

Now you might be wondering what kinds of changes you can implement in this way.

And the short answer is that it can be literally any change at all.

It doesn't matter whether it is a physical change of some kind, such as my plan to go sailing, a plan to deal with emotional habits, like my plan to stop eating chocolate, a plan to become more confident, or anything else you might imagine.

But there is a caveat: Some plans require investigation and understanding before you can implement them efficiently.

We live in a world where people have already come up with solutions for many of the problems we face and the changes we'd like to have.

This is why we had the step earlier of ensuring that the thing we want is something that someone else has achieved.

Lots of people have stopped eating chocolate, so that plan makes sense. If you don't know how habits and emotions drive the process of eating things like chocolate, it might take a while to figure out.

Thousands of people go sailing every year. It's just a matter of looking at what they do, and then adapting that to my own situation.

I could have tried to invent all those boat repair solutions myself. Doing so would have taken forever. After all, it took other people millions of years of effort to figure out how to do it. It's reasonable to suppose it would take me just as long.

Even just inventing fiberglass would probably take more than a lifetime.

By learning from others, we shortcut what might otherwise take far longer than we have into a much more manageable timeframe.

Some things might seem insurmountable at first even when others have achieved them. Especially when those things require resources we don't think we can have.

The truth is that if someone else has already done something, then most of the time so can we.

Decide what you want.

Look into how others have achieved that thing.

Make a plan to get there yourself.

Exploit your emotions to make it easy.

And then build habits to ensure that you work towards your goal.

Do not fall into the trap of thinking that you can't do it too.

# In Summary

Our minds can be considered to be composed of a conscious mind and an unconscious mind.

The part we normally see is our conscious mind, which we can use to do logic and make plans. And almost all of the human mind is unconscious. For our purposes when we want to make change, it's easiest to think of the unconscious mind as working entirely on association.

Everything we experience goes into and shapes our unconscious mind in some way. Naturally, some things are perceived as more important than others. We can use our conscious minds to drive what our unconscious minds see as important via two simple mechanisms: repetition and emotion.

Since our unconscious mind works on association, we can use some very simple strategies to start to assert control over it.

The more we do something, the more our unconscious mind will consider it to be important. Working positive emotions into things has a similar effect. Ideally we want to do both.

We have to be a little bit careful, because negative emotions tend to have a much bigger effect on us than positive ones. This means that we need to work positive emotions into the things we do as much as we can.

As a rule, we want to have many more good things than bad things in our lives.

Start to shift your focus towards the positive by keeping a hand-written journal of good things that are already in your life. Make a habit of writing in this journal at the same time every day.

This important step gives you the foot in the door. And the reality is that if we don't take the time to notice the good things we've already got, we're unlikely to benefit from adding more of them.

Next, start to shift your life itself by writing simple present-tense statements of things you'd like to be true. And then say those affirmations out loud.

This simple act causes the things we'd like to have to start occupying more of our unconscious and conscious awareness. In turn, this makes it easier to have more of those things in our lives.

A lot of our experience of the world comes from our senses, so we can ramp up the effects on our unconscious mind by visualizing the things we want as though we already have them. This allows your unconscious mind to become fully comfortable with the idea, which makes it much easier to achieve anything.

These things can be real-world physical things, like going cruising through the tropics. And they can be more mental things, such as emotions we'd like to have. It's typically a lot easier to visualize a physical goal, but the same process works just as well for emotional goals.

We can also use our conscious mind to intentionally build positive resource states and attach them to simple trigger mechanisms. This allows us to call up emotions on demand when we want to reinforce things we'd like to be doing more of. And it enables us to give ourselves little spikes of positive emotion to keep us on track with working towards our goals.

Deep trance identification can be used to automatically and unconsciously learn skills from those who are already expert at doing something you'd like to be able to do. You can even use it to reinforce the future you'd like by doing a deep trance identification with your future you.

The key with all of this is that if we want to achieve anything, we need to have our conscious mind steer things for us without using willpower any more than is absolutely required.

So do not try to consciously drive yourself towards your goals by forcing yourself to do them. Instead, find a time in your current schedule to work towards your goal, choose something you already do to act as a trigger point, then use your conscious mind to create a new habit so that every time you do that thing you're already doing, you automatically start working towards your goal.

Here's what it comes down to:

The unconscious mind works on association. It can be made to view things as being important through simple repetition and emotion. And we can use this to build habits that enable us to achieve more of the things we'd like almost on autopilot.

# Conclusion

I'd like to thank you for taking the time to make it to the end of this book. It's my hope that it has helped you.

If you've enjoyed this book, or learnt something from it, I'd really appreciate it if you could post a positive review.

This helps me out no end.

And if you're stuck on something, please feel free to reach out to me using the details on my website maxtrance.com.

It also helps me to update the book when I can see what parts don't make sense to people, which makes it better for future readers.

# Next Steps

Did you know that self-hypnosis is a useful skill to have when you'd like to supercharge your results with taming your unconscious mind?

The truth is that every concept we've covered in this book can be done without self-hypnosis. And all of them are easier and tend to work better when done from a place of self-hypnosis.

So, while you don't technically need self-hypnosis to make things work, it can help. A lot.

When we use self-hypnosis to fire up our positive emotions while writing in our gratitude journal, the effects may be magnified.

When we say our affirmations out loud from a place of self-hypnosis, they become hypnotic suggestions, and may be more deeply embedded in our mind.

Have you ever seen a hypnosis stage show where one of the subjects would do something every time the hypnotist spoke a specific word or made a specific gesture? That was a simple hypnotic trigger, which is a form of anchor. And anchors are much more effective when created from a place of hypnosis.

The same thing is true with visualizations, deep trance identification, and intentionally installing habits to help us to get more of what we want on autopilot. In every case, the mono-focus afforded by hypnosis helps.

Beyond that, it's possible to leverage self-hypnosis into experiencing hypnotic realities that seem as real as real life. And then to move from those directly into taking control of your dreams.

If you'd like to learn more about going further with self-hypnosis, including the simple process that I use to create hypnotic realities, I cover it in **The Self-Hypnosis Formula.**

# Also by Max Trance

**Artful Hypnotic Anchoring**
*My guide on how to construct and use hypnotic anchors.*

**Deep Trance Secrets**
*My guide to hypnotic fractionation and using it to generate deep trance.*

**Hypnosis Quick Start Guide**
*Step by step instructions designed to take you from complete beginner to hypnotizing your first subject.*

**Hypnosis Quick Start Workbook**
*Mostly the same as the Hypnosis Quick Start Guide, only with spaces to write out your answers to the questions I've found to be important to ask when you would like to become good at hypnosis.*

**Lucid: How to Start Lucid Dreaming Even if You Never Remember Your Dreams**
*Step by step instructions designed to take you from complete beginner to experiencing your first lucid dream and remembering it in vivid detail, even if you've never been able to recall your dreams before.*

**Lucid Dreaming Planner and Journal**
*The Dream Planner and Journal specifically designed to be used with the material in my introduction to lucid dreaming: Lucid.*

**10 More Fun Things to Do With Hypnosis**
*Additional hypnotic phenomena to use with the processes in the Hypnosis Quick Start books.*

**The Lucid Dreaming Formula: How to Wake Up Inside Your Dreams and Remember Them**

*Designed to be the quickest possible introduction to lucid dreaming, this short book covers the two essential skills that you must have if you would like to experience lucid dreams.*

**The Hypnotic Mind**

*Designed to be an overview of understanding hypnosis for beginners. Let me take you on a journey through some of the big areas of hypnosis, what they are and how they work.*

**The Self-Hypnosis Formula**

*Designed to be the quickest possible introduction to self-hypnosis, this short book covers an exact 7 step process that was engineered to guide anyone into deep self-hypnosis and teach them to use it to leap-frog into hypnotic realities, meditation, lucid dreaming, sleep, and more.*

**The Two Page Deep Trance Script**

*Want a script that I've used to quickly guide the most resistant subjects into deep hypnosis? This short script was specifically designed to do just that.*

Made in the USA
Las Vegas, NV
20 April 2024

88900617R00046